Original title:
Acorn Almanac

Copyright © 2025 Creative Arts Management OÜ
All rights reserved.

Author: Adeline Fairfax
ISBN HARDBACK: 978-1-80566-780-3
ISBN PAPERBACK: 978-1-80566-800-8

Beneath the Canopy

Beneath the trees, a squirrel pranced,
He danced around, in leaps enhanced.
With nutty jokes, he cracked a smile,
The woodland crowd laughed for a while.

A rabbit joined, and tripped on a root,
He landed flat, oh what a hoot!
The birds all chirped, they couldn't see,
A comedy act, just for the spree.

Woodland Chronicles

A wise old owl, with glasses on,
Told tales of nights till the break of dawn.
The critters gathered, all in a row,
Yet every punchline fell just so low.

A hedgehog rolled, and spouted a pun,
It was so bad, they all had to run.
But back they came, with giggles so loud,
In the forest, they formed a laugh crowd.

Seeds of Tomorrow

Little seeds hide, with giggles inside,
They whisper plans as the breeze takes a ride.
"I'll sprout a joke!" one cheeky seed said,
"Every garden needs laughter," they boldly spread.

When spring arrives, let humor bloom,
Tickling the roots, dispelling the gloom.
With roots intertwined, they all plant their cheer,
In the dance of the buds, there's nothing to fear.

The Gathering of Leaves

In autumn's grasp, the leaves conspired,
To swirl and twirl, they got all wired.
"Let's tumble down, let's make a scene!"
They fell with flair, like dancers serene.

A fox came up with quite the plan,
To catch the leaves as they fell and ran.
But tripped he did, on a twig so sly,
Now it's the leaves that laugh at the guy!

Reveries in Rust

In a world where squirrels plot,
A treasure map for the brave and hot.
They dig and dart with twinkling eyes,
For buried snacks, a sweet surprise.

Behind each tree, conspiracies bloom,
In nutty dreams where mischief can zoom.
They hoard their finds, it's all a game,
As autumn whispers their secret name.

But one bold nut, a daring fellow,
Takes a leap—becomes a yellow marshmallow.
Watch it bounce, a sight so absurd,
In the forest where laughter's heard.

So join the fun, and take a stroll,
Through a whimsical world where critters roll.
Nature's jesters, with acorns in tow,
Creating joy wherever they go.

A Symphony of Sprouts

Tiny seeds in the soil wake,
Stretching limbs for the sunshine break.
Chirping birds sing silly tunes,
Dancing leaves under the lazy moons.

A cabbage dreams of a royal crown,
While cucumbers giggle and tumble down.
Tomatoes blush with a cheeky pout,
In a garden where chaos reigns about.

The onions jest with unyielding wit,
While radishes plot a cheeky skit.
From sprouts to blooms, a joyful fuss,
In rows where laughter blooms with us.

So tap your toes in this green ballet,
As veggies waltz through the sunny day.
Nature's orchestra, both loud and spry,
As humor lingers in the sky.

Nature's Ephemeris

The calendar flips, a funny affair,
With petals today that twist in the air.
Butterflies check their whimsical flights,
As sunflowers wear silly hats at night.

The wind whispers secrets to the trees,
Tickling branches with playful breeze.
Rabbits dressed as dapper gents,
Hop through fields with no pretense.

A frog croaks a tune, chaotic and loud,
While bees buzz along, feeling quite proud.
Each day a new jest, nature's delight,
In this rollicking world, everything's right.

So glance at the leaves, with tales to share,
Each rustling whisper, a laugh in the air.
Mark your days with joy and cheer,
In the rhythms of life that draw us near.

The Language of Life

Beneath the soil, a chatter ensues,
Worms debate if it's wine or brews.
Each root extends a curious hand,
In the great underground, a funny band.

The flowers gossip in colorful hues,
Sharing tales of the morning dews.
A dandelion wishes to fly away,
While sunflowers smile, brightening the day.

Caterpillars write on leaves of green,
Their tales are wild, vibrant, and keen.
In this epic of bloom and jest,
Nature knows how to throw the best fest.

So come join the chorus, sing out loud,
In this world, where plants feel proud.
Life speaks in laughter, funny and rare,
Nature's stories float sweet in the air.

Moonlit Woodland Whispers

In the dark, the owls hoot loud,
Squirrels dance beneath the cloud.
Mice with hats and tails so fine,
Share nutty jokes with moonlit wine.

Frogs croak songs in perfect tune,
While fireflies blink like tiny moons.
The trees chuckle, branches sway,
As woodland creatures laugh and play.

A badger juggles acorns high,
While rabbits giggle as they try.
Oh what fun in the glowing night,
With woodland friends, all feeling light.

So if you wander through these woods,
Beware of tames and funny goods.
The trees are wise, their laughter real,
In moonlit nights, they spin a wheel.

The Archive of Branches

In the bark, the stories lie,
Of every gust and every sigh.
Branches shake their leafy heads,
Recalling sprightly laughs instead.

The elder tree, a wise old sage,
Tells of squirrels who stole the stage.
Nutty tales of swipes and slips,
While birds perform their feathery flips.

A token from a squirrel's heist,
An acorn cap as heady spice.
Left to gather dust and dew,
Among the leaves of every hue.

So come and peek at nature's book,
Where every nook holds a little crook.
With branches arching high above,
It's a funny tale of woodland love.

A Leaf's Legacy

A leaf once claimed it knew the best,
For jumping off the highest nest.
With a flutter and a twist,
It landed in a mushroom mist.

The tale was shared from tree to tree,
Of courage bold, wild and free.
But in the wind, it lost its flair,
And gleefully flew through the air.

The forest giggled at its plight,
As it spiraled down in sheer delight.
It settled on the ground with grace,
In stitches from the wild chase.

Now every fall is celebrated,
With each new leaf, laughter's created.
So join the fun and take a leap,
Just watch for squirrels; they're sneaky, deep.

Threads of the Treetops

The treetops weave a funny yarn,
Of squirrel parties on the lawn.
They stitch together tales of joy,
With whispers of a dancing boy.

A crow in shades of dapper style,
Cracks jokes that make the leaves compile.
With laughter echoing through the air,
As branches sway without a care.

A frisky breeze, it sweeps along,
Tickling trees with playful song.
Their threads entwined, a jolly bunch,
With acorns tossed in merry punch.

So if you find a quiet spot,
Listen in; there's laughter a lot.
The treetops share a world so wide,
Where every giggle takes a ride.

Beneath the Ancient Bough

Beneath the leafy canopy,
A squirrel lost his way,
He thought he saw a tasty nut,
But found a wig instead, hooray!

The wise old owl just chuckled low,
As branches danced with glee,
For every nut that goes awry,
Will spark some cheeky spree!

The rabbit in his fancy vest,
Would hop around in style,
He'd trade his carrots for some laughs,
And spread joy all the while.

Yet when the storm clouds gathered round,
They'd hide in roots below,
And tell tall tales of breakfast feasts,
While rain put on a show.

The Watchful Grove

In the heart of the ancient oak,
A squirrel plots his scheme,
To gather seeds and tasty treats,
And live out his grand dream.

The rabbits dance to squirrel tunes,
With twirls and leaps so grand,
While crafty birds look down with glee,
To steal snacks from their hand.

The watchful woodland critters gather,
Around the rustling leaves,
They chuckle at the silly antics,
That make them laugh till they wheeze.

But when the moonlight paints the grove,
With silver beams so bright,
They settle down for sleepy tales,
Of mischief in the night.

Chronicles of the Understory

In the shadows where secrets grow,
A bug danced on a leaf,
It slipped and slid like buttered toast,
Brought giggles, not just grief.

A hedgehog rolled into a ball,
While laughing at the prank,
He spun right into prickly plants,
And ended in a rank!

The tales of those beneath the trees,
Are filled with jests and play,
Where every bump and funny fall,
Will brighten up the day.

Each bedtime story shared at dusk,
Brings chuckles, smiles, and glee,
The chronicles of woodland life,
Are joyful as can be!

The Flight of the Squirrel

A squirrel launched from branch to branch,
Aiming for a nut,
He missed and tumbled to the ground,
And landed in a rut.

With acorn hats and woodland whirls,
They pranced without a care,
The giggles bounced through every leaf,
As laughter filled the air.

A game of tag with trees as walls,
Brought mischief to the crew,
And every leap turned into laughs,
As they chased the morning dew.

Yet as the sun began to dip,
They'd gather 'round and cheer,
For each had tales of leaps and slips,
That brought them funny cheer.

Memoirs of the Woodland Heart

In the forest, critters prance,
A squirrel took a wild chance.
Wore his acorn like a hat,
Said, "I'm the king! Now where's my cat?"

Nuts fell down like raindrops bright,
Squirrels squealed in pure delight.
A dance-off with the foxes near,
The forest echoed, full of cheer!

A beaver brought a floating log,
Declared it hip—just like a frog.
The owls hooted, "What a sight!"
As dances turned to an uproarious night!

When bedtime came, the forest yawned,
Squirrel snuggled deep, but dawn's not dawned.
With dreams of nuts and silly fun,
The woodland party had just begun!

Seasons Beneath the Bark

Winter's chill had stirred the trees,
A squirrel slipped—oh, such a tease!
He thought he'd glide on ice so slick,
But fell with a thud, now that's the trick!

Spring arrived with blooms in tow,
Bunnies hopping to and fro.
With flowers bright, they all conspired,
To whip up salads, much admired!

Summer sun, a blazing prank,
A raccoon swam in the river's bank.
He fished for snacks, with cheeky flair,
But caught his tail, now isn't that rare?

Autumn's leaves danced 'round the crowd,
Chasing winds, they laughed out loud.
With harvest moons and cider cheer,
The critters sang, "Let's party here!"

In the Shadow of Giants

Beneath the oaks, the shadows play,
A tiny mouse spins tales of sway.
"I'm bigger than a crumb!" he shouts,
As all his friends just laugh, no doubts!

A rabbit hops and waves his ears,
Claims he hides from cookies near.
When toasted treats come near his hutch,
He dances like it's all too much!

The old oak cracked a wise old joke,
About a squirrel who learned to poke.
"Why did you climb all that high?"
He answered, "To see the cookie pie!"

With sunlight spilling through the leaves,
The critters come and share their dreams.
In shadows tall, they share their glee,
And giggle on with wild esprit!

Roots and Revelations

In the underbrush, wise roots cling,
Whispering tales of every spring.
"Did you hear that?" the faun inquired,
"Bramble said he's even inspired!"

The flowers raised their heads so proud,
"We're the prettiest in the crowd!"
A dandelion blew with flourishing flair,
"But I've got seeds that float in the air!"

The hedgehog snoozed beneath a shade,
Dreaming of the pranks he played.
When morning came, he'd pop up quick,
With a tiny dance and a silly flick!

Tails wiggled, paws tapped to the beat,
Each critter's heart, a little fleet.
In the roots, where tales unfurl,
They laughed and played, what a whimsical world!

Echoes of the Rustic Realm

In the woods, a squirrel's dance,
Spinning tales, it takes a chance,
With a flick and a leap, oh so spry,
Chasing shadows of the sky.

A wise old owl, with glasses neat,
Scrutinizing every little beet,
"Why do they try to cross my path?"
He chuckles, finishing his math.

The bumblebee, in grand parade,
Buzzing loud, his role displayed,
"I bring the honey, oh what a treat!"
Makes the daisies sway to the beat.

And in the grass, a cricket plays,
Noisy nights bring endless praise,
"When the moon shines, we hold the show,"
Performing for stars, they put on a glow.

The Gathering of Time

The clock ticks slow in kiwi vines,
While chubby rabbits switch up signs,
"Let's hop to it, don't be late!"
Time's just a concept, we'll celebrate!

Old tortoises in their shells,
Tell stories of magical spells,
"I took a nap for just one year,"
"But woke up fresh! Oh dear! Oh dear!"

The fox tips his hat with flair,
"I'm the best-dressed—beyond compare!"
He struts on by, a dapper sight,
But trips on roots, oh what a fright!

Beneath the moon, the owls convene,
Judging who's the silliest seen,
With feathered friends in laughter's grasp,
As day breaks, they still can't unclasp.

Folklore of the Forest Floor

Gather 'round for tales of cheer,
Where mushrooms giggle without fear,
A hedgehog spins a yarn so wild,
Even the wise trees are beguiled.

The raccoon dons a mask in style,
His thievery brings quite a smile,
"I steal your snacks, but just for fun,"
He winks and scampers, on the run!

Tales of beavers building dams,
Who think they're artists, here's who jams,
"Look at our masterpiece, so grand!"
Then the rain comes, they start to stand!

A porcupine rolls with glee,
"I'm the spikiest, can't you see?"
While ants in line march to and fro,
They're planning a party with quite a show!

Beneath the Golden Canopy

Beneath the leaves, a dance unfolds,
With whispers of laughter and stories told,
A group of rabbits in a conga line,
Flopping to rhythms so divine.

A butterfly flutters with a fancy flair,
"Catch me if you can!" floats in the air,
The flowers giggle, swaying fast,
"You'll need some luck, but not too vast!"

In the twilight, a lizard preens,
"I'm stunning!" he shouts, while grooming his greens,
Chasing his tail, oh what a sight,
While fireflies dance, lighting the night.

And as dawn breaks, all heads will bow,
To the sun peeking over, "Oh wow!"
With joy in their hearts and smiles so wide,
They greet the morning, full of pride.

Reverie of the Roots

In the garden, roots do dance,
Laughing at the squirrel's prance.
Worms wear ties for silly fun,
As sunlight sparkles, just begun.

Rabbits wear their Sunday best,
While daisies throw a flower fest.
The carrots joke with leafy greens,
About their dreams of movie scenes.

A sneaky fox in shades of brown,
Claims he's the king of this small town.
Roots giggle softly underground,
While wild tales of mischief abound.

In this world of whimsy bright,
Laughter echoes day and night.
Oh, what fun the roots contrive,
In a giggly earth, so alive!

The Embrace of Earth

Underneath the leafy crown,
Earth gives hugs, it won't back down.
Worms will wiggle, squirrels will tease,
And ants march by with such great ease.

A clamoring chorus, bugs unite,
As crickets sing to stars at night.
While daisies whisper cheeky tales,
Of owls who wear their funny veils.

The soil dreams of sandwich fare,
With each layer, banter rare.
Mice throw cheese parties, oh so grand,
As frogs jump in a funky band.

In this wondrous, earthy jest,
Nature's giggles never rest.
With roots entwined and sprouting glee,
It's a funny world beneath the tree!

Ecstasy of the Evergreen

Pine trees sway with a silly cheer,
Tickling raccoons near and dear.
With every gust, they sway and bend,
Reminding all to fully blend.

A porcupine, with spiky flair,
Tries to dance in the open air.
The squirrels chuckle, tails a-twitch,
As branches rattle, quite the pitch.

Winter coats of white do fall,
Snowflakes giggle, heed the call.
With snowmen dancing, hats askew,
The evergreens join in the view.

In this forest, jokes abound,
Life is lively all around.
Nature's laughter fills the air,
In a world we love to share!

Dusty Trails and Twilit Tales

On dusty trails where shadows play,
Funny creatures roam and sway.
Bumblebees gossip, whisper low,
As twilight's glow begins to show.

A raccoon with a curious grin,
Plans an adventure with a spin.
He drags along his clumsy friend,
A turtle dragging till the end.

Together they stroll under the moon,
Singing a silly, joyful tune.
The owls wink in the soft night air,
As shadows dance—a quirky flair.

Tales are spun of fables clear,
With laughter held and friends so dear.
Under starlit skies, they weave,
A tapestry of jokes to leave!

Fables of the Forest

In the woods, where squirrels play,
A bear plays hopscotch every day.
Trees gossip, whisper secrets low,
While raccoons dance in a moonlit glow.

The owls wear glasses, so wise and sage,
They read the forest from a worn-out page.
Chipmunks hold court, they each take a seat,
Debating whose nuts are the best kind to eat.

A fox loves to wear a bright purple hat,
He claims it's the fashion, imagine that!
The mushrooms giggle, they can't keep it down,
When the porcupine rolls, he steals the crown.

The trees sway and laugh, all in good cheer,
While the bunnies sing tunes for all to hear.
With nonsense and joy, they fill the air,
In the fables of the forest, life's rare and fair.

Dreams in the Dust

In a corner of the world, dreams unfold,
Where beetles spin yarns, both silly and bold.
Ladybugs race on little toy cars,
While crickets strum tunes beneath the stars.

A dandelion wishes on a soft breeze,
Confessing to ants, 'I'm not just a tease!'
Grasshoppers giggle, attempting to sing,
Their legs in a tangle, it's quite the thing!

The dust gathers tales of the day and night,
Where shadows play tag until morning light.
Mice tell stories with sneezes and puffs,
While hedgehogs chuckle, their laughter is tough.

Dreams in the dust are a comical treat,
With winks and nods, the fun is complete.
Nature's own circus, a lively affair,
With whispers and giggles swaying in air.

Secrets of the Seed

Deep in the earth, secrets are kept,
Where worms make a bed, and seedlings are swept.
A sunflower whispers, 'I'm tall and I shine,'
While radishes giggle at the grapevines divine.

The roots hold meetings in the cool, dark ground,
Where truths of the garden are joyfully found.
Pumpkins declare, with a crown on their head,
'We're royalty here, in our orange thread!'

The breeze tells stories as it rustles leaves,
With laughter and mischief, each secret deceives.
Epic tales spin from the petals that sway,
As bees buzz along, in frolicsome play.

Secrets of the seed, oh, what a delight,
With mischief and joy, day turns into night.
Life's little treasures, in every small deed,
Bloom in the laughter of nature's own creed.

Tales of Timber and Time

Once in the woods, a tree lost its shoe,
It searched high and low but found just dew.
A woodpecker chuckled from a branch up high,
'Timber's in trouble! Oh my, oh my!'

Log cabins giggle, with stories to tell,
Of squirrels who skateboard and credits as well.
Branches join in with a raucous old jive,
As the logs stage dances, keeping time alive.

The shadows do pirouettes under the sun,
Tick-tock they go, oh what silly fun!
The owls hold a contest of who can blink best,
While rabbits take turns, in dance-offs, they jest.

Tales of timber run wild and free,
Where laughter echoes, as sweet as can be.
In every creak and crack of the wood,
Lies a history etched, misunderstood.

Whispers of the Oak

In the forest, a squirrel debates,
If the nuts are his or his buddy's fate.
A dance of the leaves, a rustle, a shout,
"Hey, where'd my stash go?" a hungry pout.

Old branches creak with stories to share,
Of acorns that fell with not one ounce of care.
The raccoon just laughs, counting all his gains,
While a wise old owl feigns to ignore the pains.

The wind plays tricks, it's frolicking near,
Leaves swirl in jest, oh, what a cheer!
A chipmunk capers, all fluff and delight,
Building a fortress with nuts in sight.

Beneath the grand oak, the laughter is bright,
As nature's own jesters revel in light.
In this woodland circus, nothing feels stale,
Life's just a punchline, on nature's grand scale.

Autumn's Knotted Secrets

Under the branches where shadows swell,
A mouse tells tales, oh wouldn't you tell?
Of the gnome who hid in a hollowed-out stump,
With a mustache made out of an acorn's plump.

Forget-me-not flowers join in the fun,
As bees buzz by, laughing, 'Aren't we the ones?'
The breeze carries giggles 'neath flickering light,
As pumpkins grow grinning, all merry and bright.

Bumbled bees in a tangled conundrum,
Trying to poach honey, they look so glum.
"Do you have any nuts?" one bumblebee queries,
While raccoons plot mischief, stirring up series.

So autumn unfolds, in whispers and grins,
Keeping close secrets as laughter begins.
With a spark of delight in the air all around,
In the tangled-up woods, pure joy can be found.

Beneath the Canopy of Time

In a garden of giggles, a seed takes flight,
Wondering loudly, "Am I left or right?"
With roots that twist and tangle in thrift,
The worms roll their eyes, saying, "What a gift!"

As the sun stretches wide, and shadows conspire,
A rabbit writes memoirs about the wild fire.
"Got lost in the weeds, oh, what a plight!
But found a nice patch to nap through the night."

Chipmunks trade tales of their grand escapade,
As caterpillars bask in the grand masquerade.
The forest is buzzing with giggles galore,
With secrets unspooling through every door.

So beneath the tall trees, old stories unfurl,
In this merry playground, the fun starts to whirl.
With laughter a-sway, and spirits that climb,
Nature is cheeky, oh, how we all rhyme!

The Seedling Chronicles

Sprouting with mischief, a seedling takes hold,
Boasting of stories, both timid and bold.
"I'm destined for greatness!" it yells to the sky,
While a wise old snail just rolls by with a sigh.

Leaves rustle softly, sharing their dreams,
In a competitive race, they burst at the seams.
The dandelion giggles, with fluff on its head,
"Don't take it so serious, let's party instead!"

Beneath the bright canopy, friends join the fray,
As shadows play tricks throughout the warm day.
The flowers turn faces, with petals that cheer,
Celebrating each other, with laughter sincere.

So join in the fun, let your worries uncoil,
In this merry garden, you're free of toil.
With stories unfolding in twirls and in bends,
The seedling's adventure is where joy transcends.

A Tapestry of Timber Tales

In the forest where the squirrels play,
Chasing dreams on a sunny day.
A nut parade, oh what a sight!
They dance around with sheer delight.

From twig to twig, they leap and bound,
In their world, laughter is profound.
With capes of leaves, they take their flight,
And giggle hard through day and night.

The wise old owl hoots a tune,
While raccoons waltz beneath the moon.
Each branch a stage, each tree a friend,
In this tapestry that has no end.

So join the fun, don't be a bore!
Nature's antics leave us wanting more.
In every rustle, hear the cheer,
For timber tales bring joy and beer!

Whispers of Oak

Beneath the branches, secrets swirl,
As playful breezes begin to twirl.
Leaves rustle, and giggles arise,
From the wise old oak with twinkling eyes.

The critters gather for a grand feast,
With acorns aplenty, at least!
A feast of laughter, a buffet of fun,
As shadows stretch beneath the sun.

The tree tells stories of days gone by,
Of sneaky foxes who danced on high.
With every creak, it shares a jest,
So come, my friends, you'll be impressed!

In the world of whispers, joy takes flight,
With oak-shaped jokes that feel just right.
So lend an ear and join the cheer,
For timber's tale can brighten a year!

The Seedling's Journey

A little seedling sprouted one day,
With big dreams of reaching the Milky Way.
It stretched its leaves and waved its roots,
"Look at me! I'm the tree that hoots!"

The ants marched by with a tiny drum,
"Grow, dear sprout! You're sure to come!"
The beetles clapped with every beat,
A lively tune beneath its feet.

It dreamed of branches both wide and tall,
And silly songbirds that might just call.
"I'm the king of the garden!" it would shout,
While dandelions flicked it about.

Through rain and sun, it laughed and played,
In the soil of dreams where fun was laid.
And though it's small, it spreads its cheer,
For even tiny seeds can persevere!

Echoes of Autumn

As autumn rolls in with a rustling sound,
Pumpkins giggle as they spin 'round.
Leaves dance down in a colorful swirl,
The trees drop jokes, oh what a twirl!

Squirrels in hats collect their loot,
While critters swap tales in their harvest suit.
The breeze carries laughter, leaps through the air,
Nature's stage where no one's quite bare.

With every crunch beneath our feet,
We chase off the chill with laughter sweet.
For the echoes of autumn bring a playful quirk,
Where mischief abounds, and giggles lurk.

So gather 'round, let the fun unfold,
In the golden light, as stories are told.
Echoes of joy, as seasons collide,
In the heart of autumn, let laughter reside!

The Gentle Transition

The leaves are laughing, turning gold,
As squirrels dance, so brave and bold.
They twitch and stretch, like shorts at noon,
Chasing shadows, singing tunes.

The breeze is tickling the branches high,
While little birds are learning to fly.
With every flap, there's giggles loud,
Nature's mischief, a lively crowd.

Chubby squirrels forgot their fill,
Their cheeks puffed up, they dash, they spill.
In every corner, a comedy crew,
Nature's playhouse, all for you!

As daylight fades and stars appear,
The critters chuckle, without a fear.
For in this forest, with fun abound,
The funny games will always resound.

Roots and Revelations

The roots are whispering under ground,
Secrets and stories, all around.
A gopher snickers, 'What's the fuss?'
His underground club, a real plus!

A chipmunk claims the title of king,
With acorns as jewels, they all bling.
He holds a court, but fumbles treats,
What a scene! The laughter, it beats!

The mushrooms giggle, sporting their hats,
In vibrant colors, like playful brats.
With every spore, they spread the cheer,
In this fun world, all are near.

By dusk, they gather for one last show,
Jokes and jests, with a radiant glow.
In the woods, where laughter's the law,
Roots reveal joy, in every flaw.

Under the Watchful Sky

Beneath the blue, a parade starts,
With beetles doing their funny arts.
They march in line, they twist and shout,
While thinking they're what it's all about.

A wise old owl, perched with grace,
Rolls his eyes at the frenzied race.
'Why dance so hard?' he hoots with glee,
'Just chill with me, and sip some tea!'

A fox prances by in roller blades,
'Look at me!'—he strikes silly aids.
But trips on roots, does a clumsy flip,
The forest echoes with laughter's grip.

As clouds drift by, a playful sight,
The sun peeks through, turns day to night.
Creatures join in, with glad delight,
Under the sky, everything feels right.

The Pulse of the Forest

The bouncy beat of the forest floor,
Squirrels jump like they're at a store.
They shuffle and shake, in wild display,
'Who knew getting nuts could be so fey?'

The rabbits hop with an acrobat's flair,
Twisting mid-air, causing a scare.
'Oh dear!' they gasp, 'Not again, Fred!'
The punchline lies in a lettuce bed.

With whirls and twirls, the insects sing,
In harmony, their buzzing takes wing.
A caterpillar offering to break dance,
Insect rhythms lead to their chance.

As twilight creeps, the fun's not done,
Fireflies gather, the evening's fun.
With every flicker, a daring race,
In this vibrant world, joy finds its place.

Secrets in the Soil

Tiny treasures tucked away,
Beneath the roots where critters play.
Worms gossip about their finds,
Whispering secrets, oh so kind.

Nuts and snacks in earthy beds,
Hosting parties for the shreds.
Squirrels dance with acorn glee,
Gathering snacks, oh so carefree.

Earthworms dream of leafy treats,
Planning feasts with crunchy sweets.
Nature's whispers fill the air,
Laughter dances everywhere.

Digging deep with tiny paws,
Mischief reigns without a pause.
Life unfolds in playful jest,
Secrets hidden in their nest.

Threads of Sunlight and Shade

Sunbeams tickle leaves so bright,
While shadows play tag, what a sight!
Laughter ripples in the breeze,
Nature's game among the trees.

Dappled light and silly sounds,
Squirrels mimic roundabouts.
Chasing rays, they dart and weave,
Creating laughs, you wouldn't believe!

Beneath the boughs, a gathering forms,
Where friendship triumphs 'gainst all norms.
Joking jays with raucous calls,
Bring cheer that never falls.

In this dance of light and shade,
Every creature has it made.
Sunlit threads, a woven quilt,
A fabric of laughter, joy is built.

Cartography of the Canopy

Above the world, a tangled map,
Where branches twist and critters nap.
Squirrels plot their daring routes,
While wise old owls lay down their truths.

Each limb a road, each leaf a sign,
Navigating with a cheeky grin.
Raccoons consult their secret charts,
Adventuring with crafty hearts.

Pine cones mark the treasure zones,
A banquet where the squirrel moans.
With acorn stashes, they sing their praise,
Of jumping high in playful ways.

Branches bridge the skies of blue,
Mapping mischief for a crew.
Up in the heights, the laughter swells,
Creating stories only nature tells.

Legends Carved in Wood

Tall tales carved on sturdy bark,
Tell of journeys through the dark.
Whispered myths of squirrel lore,
Echo under branches galore.

Knots and twists, the stories grow,
With knobby faces all aglow.
Each tree holds laughter, mischief, and cheer,
As woodland critters gather near.

Oaken seats for tales to share,
Where every creature shows they care.
From chipmunks to the wise old deer,
All retreat to listen here.

Carved in wood, their voices soar,
Legends bloom forevermore.
In this forest, tales entwine,
A world where joy and fun align.

The Scribe of Seasons

In autumn's grip, the squirrels dance,
With tiny hats, they take a chance.
They gather nuts, a silly spree,
As leaves let go, quite carelessly.

The winter's chill brings snowy hats,
They build a fort to block the cats.
With every snowball, giggles rise,
As snowmen wear the silliest ties.

Then spring arrives with flowers bright,
The bunnies bounce in pure delight.
They hop along and tease the bee,
"Why buzz around, when you could flee?"

By summer's time, with sun ablaze,
They've turned the yard into a maze.
With tiny shorts, they run and twirl,
These seasonal scribes, a comic whirl.

Whispers in the Wind

The wind confesses secrets sly,
To branches swaying, oh so high.
"Did you hear what the flowers said?"
"Just bloom and dance, forget your bed!"

A leaf replied with a rustling grin,
"Let's play tag before we thin!"
With every gust, the laughter flies,
As whispers curl 'neath sunny skies.

The breeze invites the critters near,
"Join in our game, bring your cheer!"
A mouse with shades begins to groove,
While sparrows sing and squirrels move.

Their joy cascades with nature's song,
It's fun to see who hops along.
A dance of whispers, all in jest,
In every gust, they find their fest.

Shadows Beneath the Bough

Beneath the bough, the shadows play,
With creatures creeping on their way.
A turtle in his shell takes rest,
While ants march on, they're quite the jest!

A wise old owl blinks in delight,
"Who's ready for a game tonight?"
The shadows giggle, start to sway,
As starry twinkles join the fray.

A raccoon masks his sneaky face,
As everyone prepares to race.
They dash around like silly fools,
In this enchantment, laughter rules!

When moonlight spills on leafy ground,
A harmony of joy is found.
In shadows cast, pure fun takes flight,
Under the boughs, all feels just right.

The Quiet Evolution

In nature's course, a change does creep,
Where crickets chirp and branches leap.
The flowers nod with gentle grace,
As bees all rush, in silly chase.

A caterpillar dons a cape,
"I'll soar one day, no need to scrape!"
But first, it munches every leaf,
With veggie dreams beyond belief.

The frogs in ponds, with leaps so bold,
Share tales of sunsets, joys untold.
They croak about their heroic quests,
With whimsical tales that never rest.

Evolving thoughts in the warm embrace,
Of sunbeams dancing, a lighted space.
Through every change, they find their flair,
In quiet evolution, laughter's air.

The Heartbeat of the Hollow

In the hollow where the squirrels play,
A nutty dance starts every day.
They twirl and twist without a care,
While birds chuckle from their airy lair.

A chipmunk wears a tiny hat,
And struts around like he's a cat.
The owl hoots out a laugh so grand,
As the ants form up a marching band.

The breeze brings tales of daffodils,
With jokes that tickle and give you thrills.
The laughter in the glen does swell,
As nature spins its silly spell.

So come and join this woodland cheer,
Where every critter brings good cheer.
The hollow beats with joy so sweet,
Come dance along to nature's beat!

Chronicles Among the Roots

Down below where the shadows crawl,
The roots argue, oh the tales they sprawl!
A willow claims it's the tallest tree,
While the daisies giggle at its vanity.

A hedgehog pens a gossip's tome,
Writes of badgers who won't stay home.
The shrooms gather for a midnight feast,
And claim they've caught a ghostly beast!

The wise old tortoise shares his lore,
Of three-legged frogs who swam ashore.
Each root, a tale, a giggle or two,
In this library where branches grew.

So lend an ear to those underground,
In the party of whispers and laughter found.
For every twist and turn's a quip,
In the chronicles where our friendships grip.

Glimpses of Green

In the meadow, colors flash and gleam,
Life's a carnival—a wild dream!
The grasshoppers jump and make a fuss,
While butterflies giggle on a big, bright bus.

Beneath a leaf, a snail stirs slow,
Complaining why he can't run like the crow.
He dreams of a race on a glossy track,
While ladybugs giggle, "Oh, there's no lack!"

The daisies gossip with a sunny side,
About the clouds that often hide.
"Look at that squirrel, what a nutty tease,
Pretending to climb those wobbly trees!"

With every laugh, a sparkle grows,
In glimpses of green, where mischief flows.
Join the fun, let your spirits soar,
For life in the meadow opens many a door!

The Nest of Time

In twisted branches high and wide,
There's a nest where giggles bide.
With feathers piled so soft and warm,
A cozy spot from any storm.

The bluebirds sing of what they miss,
A worm that dodged a peck or kiss.
They reminisce with flapping wings,
While the woodpecker loudly rings.

The passage of time, there's fun to see,
What's next? A party? A cup of tea?
The squirrels gather to scheme and plot,
On how to snag the best of what's hot.

In this nest, the laughter grows,
As friends swap tales in endless throes.
For each memory is a cherished rhyme,
Nestled quietly in the arms of time.

The Voice of the Vines

In the garden, vines do chatter,
Spilling secrets, nothing's the matter.
They plot and they plan, a grape escape,
Whispering tales, in their leafy cape.

A squabble breaks out, the peas get loud,
While carrots stand tall, far too proud.
The herbs start a dance, they twirl and sway,
Chasing away all the clouds of gray.

They mock the tomatoes, too juicy to speak,
While radishes giggle, their roots in a streak.
Laughter erupts, as they twine and mix,
A jolly old time, in their green bag of tricks.

So if you're in need of a laugh or a cheer,
Just visit the vines, they'll bring good cheer.
A garden of joy, where jokes intertwine,
With rhythm and rhyme, they're simply divine.

Paths of Promise

The path is winding with chocolate chunks,
Beneath my feet, a dance of trunks.
Squeaky squirrels in top hats trot,
Promising wonders with every plot.

Berries boast of flavors so wild,
While mushrooms giggle, like a playful child.
Beneath the bushes, a gnome takes a nap,
Dreaming of snacks from an ancient map.

Each step is a riddle, a giggle in tow,
Where carrots recite, and lettuce bestow.
The wind plays a tune, of whimsy and joy,
As we stroll along, girl and boy.

So come take the journey, it's silly and bright,
With laughs in the air and the moon shining white.
Each path beckons laughter, a cheeky delight,
Leading us onward through day and the night.

The Legacy of Loam

In the soil so rich, the gossip will flow,
Of worms that do wiggle and critters that glow.
The legacy here is a playful tease,
As roots intertwine in a dance such as these.

Every shovel full, a tale to be told,
Of beetles and bugs, eternally bold.
The daisies get tipsy on sunshine and dew,
While dandelions puff, their wishes come true.

A ladybug squeaks, 'I rule this plot!'
While spiders weave stories in webs of thought.
With laughter and joy, the garden unearths,
A legacy built on the silliness of births.

So dig in the loam, where quirks come alive,
In a world where the fun just continues to thrive.
Every grain holds a memory, laughter, and cheer,
In this earthy playground, let's shout it out clear!

The Sighs of the Saplings

The saplings stretch with a giggly sigh,
Reaching for clouds as they fling high.
Their whispers fill the breeze with cheer,
"Look at us grow, we've nothing to fear!"

With leaves a-flutter, they dance in the sun,
Each swish and sway, a joke just begun.
One suggests a tickle, another a tease,
While nearby the daisies just laugh with glee.

A wise old oak listens and hums along,
While laughing woodpeckers sing a sweet song.
"Let's have a party," the spruces decree,
"A gathering of giggles, just wait and see!"

The saplings unite, their roots intertwine,
Beneath them, the soil feels lively and fine.
In a world full of chuckles, they reach for the sky,
With dreams that are funny and hopes that fly high.

Nature's Tiny Timekeepers

In the forest depths, time ticks slow,
Squirrels play games, with no place to go.
Trees whisper gossip, like old chums do,
As the sun races past, in a sky so blue.

Fungi hold meetings, in their mossy coat,
Debating the virtues of each little boat.
Mushrooms wear hats, all sprout with glee,
While ladybugs count leaves, one-two-three.

Chipmunks in bow ties, shuffle in line,
Preparing their speeches for the grand design.
In the woodsy school, laughter fills the air,
Nature's tiny timekeepers, with style and flair.

Little wonders play tricks, just to amuse,
To tickle our thoughts, and lighthearted views.
With each passing moment, they keep us in check,
In this whimsical realm, we're all on deck!

The Wisdom Beneath the Leaf

Under the canopy, wisdom prevails,
With whispers of winds, and tall-tale trails.
Frogs sing in chorus, wise beyond years,
While crickets give lectures, and capture our cheers.

Beneath every leaf, a secret is kept,
Stories of sunlight, where shadows have crept.
The ants hold a conference, plans in the air,
While owls roll their eyes, in feathery glare.

From roots deep in earth to tips high above,
Nature shares secrets wrapped up in love.
So gather your thoughts in gusts of delight,
Find wisdom in laughter; it's always in sight.

A squirrel missed breakfast, decided to dance,
While hedgehogs rolled past, in their spiky pants.
In this leafy domain, humor runs wild,
Where nature's the teacher, and every step's styled!

Chronicles of the Evergreen

In evergreen groves, tales twist and turn,
As pine needles giggle, and sap starts to churn.
Squirrels pen stories, with nuts as their ink,
While owls script sagas, reminders to think.

Trees swap their secrets, with gnarled old barks,
Discussing the mischief of runaway larks.
The tales of the forest, both silly and grand,
In this book of the wild, they take their stand.

With every new season, a chapter unfolds,
From shady ambitions to bold stories told.
The breeze writes the ending, both merry and bright,
In the chronicles where all endings feel right.

So join in the fun, let laughter ignite,
Among evergreens dressed in magical light.
Nature's tall storytellers, stand tall and sing,
In the chronicles where joy, like a melody, clings!

Starlit Stories of the Underbrush

In the underbrush deep, where shadows reside,
Fireflies gather and stars wink with pride.
Each flicker's a word, in the night's gentle rhyme,
As whispers of critters dance free through the time.

Crickets compose symphonies, rich and profound,
While raccoons debate who makes the best sound.
A hedgehog spins tales of adventures gone by,
With every new twinkle, the night draws a sigh.

Mice in their slippers, tiptoe with grace,
Sharing the secrets of the starlit space.
Beneath the lush canopy, laughter does spring,
In the underbrush kingdom, where joy's everything.

So if you find trouble, and need some cheer,
Head to the brush, let your worries disappear.
With starlit stories, our spirits will bloom,
In the glow of the night, feel your heart resume!

Songs of the Shadows

In the dark, the squirrels play,
Twirling leaves in silly ballet.
Mice are plotting, oh what fun,
They'll steal the snacks when day is done.

The owls hoot in giggling glee,
Chasing bugs and climbing trees.
A raccoon's dance, a silly sight,
Underneath the pale moonlight.

With shadows stretching, they all prance,
Doing their best to join the dance.
A leaf spins down, a funny twist,
Nature's party, you can't resist!

As dawn breaks, the antics cease,
All settle down for some sweet peace.
But wait! What's that? Oh, what a mess,
Nature's humor—what a stress!

Footprints in the Foliage

Tiny prints on leaves unfold,
Squirrels racing, oh so bold.
A muddy track from toe to tail,
Leads to trouble, I won't tell a tale.

Follow the trail, you might just find,
A treasure buried, one of a kind.
But wait! It's just an acorn lost,
The excitement fades, oh what a cost!

With every step, the laughter grows,
Tiny critters strike funny poses.
A fox trips up, a grand old fall,
Raccoons giggle, and that's not all.

Nature's clues, all piled high,
Do you wonder who and why?
From tiny feet, they play their game,
In the foliage, it's all the same!

Chronicles of Cold Winds

When winter blows, they bundle tight,
Critters dodging, quite the sight.
A hedgehog rolls, a warm embrace,
While snowflakes dance, they keep the pace.

The chill brings laughter, jokes to share,
With snowball fights, all in the air.
Birds wear hats made from old socks,
And squirrels try on shoes like clocks!

One windy day, a kite takes flight,
A treetop chase, what pure delight.
Fluffy tails and squeaky cheers,
They spin and tumble, faced with fears.

As night falls, the chill subsides,
Nature's play, where joy abides.
With stars above, they cozy down,
In frosty silence, smiles abound!

Nestled in Nature's Nook

In a nook, where laughter dwells,
A family of bunnies ring their bells.
Tales of mischief, they share in glee,
While munching on grass, oh can it be?

A squirrel ambushes, what a trick!
Dodging swift, and oh so quick!
A tiny mess, the acorns fly,
Their comedy show makes all squirrels sigh.

As sunlight whispers through the trees,
A cozy spot—the best of degrees.
A chipmunk juggles seeds galore,
While a wise old owl begins to snore.

When shadows fade, and day is done,
Their giggles echo, oh what fun!
In nature's cradle, laughter blooms,
Nestled safe, in leafy rooms.

Nature's Personal Ledger

In the woods, a squirrel's glee,
Counting nuts, one, two, three.
Juggling acorns, quite a sight,
He'll miss the branch and take a flight!

Beneath the oaks, he finds his stash,
'These are mine!' he says with panache.
A feathered thief gives a sly glance,
'You think you'll keep them? Not a chance!'

The hedgehog, rolling, joins the fun,
Looking for bugs, oh what a run!
The trees above give a little shake,
As giggles echo, make no mistake!

So keep your secrets, keep them tight,
Nature's giggle fills the night.
For every critter has a dream,
To hoard their treasure and scheme!

The Dance of the Pines

Pines prance in the gentle breeze,
Whispering secrets with such ease.
Beneath the boughs, wee critters sway,
Joining the trees in a playful ballet.

A woodpecker taps out a catchy beat,
While chipmunks wiggle on tiny feet.
The branches sway, a rhythm divine,
Nature's dance floor, all intertwined!

As sunlight splashes through the green,
A party scene like you've never seen.
Twisting and turning, oh what a sight,
Pines shake their needles, pure delight!

And when the moon begins to rise,
The curtain drops, to our surprise.
Yet in the still of the starry night,
Nature smirks, 'We'll dance till light!'

Harvest of Hues

Autumn paints with a silly brush,
Orange and yellow in a wild rush.
Leaves pirouette, so bold and bright,
Chasing the wind with pure delight.

A pumpkin tells a corny joke,
While apples giggle at a smoky oak.
Crisp air carries a playful tease,
Nature's laughter is sure to please!

The squash parade rolls down the hill,
'Who will taste me?' it shouts with thrill.
Colors clash in a joyful way,
As the harvest keeps the blues at bay!

So gather 'round, let's celebrate,
With pies and cider, isn't it great?
In this montage, we find our place,
In the wild hues of nature's embrace!

The Language of Leaves

Leaves chatter softly, gossiping trees,
'You heard about the crow? He's got quite the tease!'
Rustling softly, in breezy plays,
Decoding whispers in sunny rays.

A beetle struts in a tiny tux,
While ladybugs gossip like a bunch of ducks.
'Who's the brightest of us all?'
Leaves puff up, enjoying the call.

A rustle here, a flutter there,
Leaves communicate with flair and care.
The dance of colors, a vibrant spree,
Nature's comedy, come laugh with me!

So listen close to the woodland talk,
Where every shade of green will walk.
Life's a jest in this leafy maze,
Join in the fun, and share the praise!

Tales from the Forest Floor

In the green where squirrels play,
A cat fell in, much to its dismay.
It chased a leaf, went spinning round,
And bumped its head on the soft, damp ground.

A worm with glasses reads the news,
While ants discuss their dancing shoes.
A butterfly jumps, declares it's spry,
And flutters off to a tea that's nearby.

A rabbit in a vest makes quite a scene,
Telling jokes that only grass can glean.
The mushrooms giggle; it's quite a show,
As the wind whispers why they just grow.

And here's the secret, the forest keeps,
It holds the laughter as the old tree sleeps.
Beneath its boughs, fun stories are spun,
Where every critter knows how to have fun.

Echoes of the Ancient Trees

An oak so wise, with stories old,
Told tales of knots and leaves of gold.
His laughter echoed through every bough,
As squirrels played 'Guess Who' right then and now.

A willow weeps, but it's all a show,
For beneath her branches, the wildflowers grow.
She sways and whispers silly chants,
While dandelions dance in their bright summer pants.

The pine cones joke about wishful dreams,
And plan their pranks on passing streams.
A chipmunk serves lemonade with charm,
As trees fall silent, enjoying the calm.

So gather 'round if you wish to see,
The shenanigans of this forest spree.
For each trunk and twig has a tale to share,
Of giggles and grins that float through the air.

A Gathering of Dreams

Nighttime falls, the stars take stage,
The critters gather, wise and sage.
A fox tells stories of moonlit strolls,
While fireflies twinkle like vibrant coals.

The badger brings snacks, oh what a treat!
Edible wonders, both savory and sweet.
They munch on mushrooms, and giggles arise,
As a raccoon shows off in a silly disguise.

An owl with glasses keeps track of time,
And hoots in rhythm, bizarre yet sublime.
Each tale gets taller, each laugh gets loud,
While branches sway, joining the crowd.

As dawn approaches, they bid adieu,
With dreams of tomorrows, oh so askew!
So sleep with glee, let your thoughts entwine,
For the forest's heart has a beat so fine.

The Nut-Bearing Sky

The sky above, a nutty delight,
Squirrels look up with hearts full of flight.
"Oh dear," said one, with a comical frown,
"Did you see the clouds just falling down?"

He caught a walnut, gave it a toss,
While a chipmunk danced, declaring no loss.
"Next time, let's see if we can make stew,
From the fluffy clouds that float up there too!"

A nut rain's coming, or so they boast,
As they prepare for the craziest toast.
They stack up the nuts, a wobbly pile,
Then slip and slide in a wild forest style.

So under the sky, where giggles abound,
They play with nature, and joy is found.
With each nut that falls, together they cheer,
For the fun-loving forest, let's keep it near!

Ancestral Echoes in Moss

In the forest, whispers laugh,
Roots entangled, share their path.
Old trees gossip, branches sway,
Beneath the canopy, they play.

Moss becomes a cozy seat,
Where fungi and critters meet.
Squirrels tell tales of acrobats,
While wise old owls wear their hats.

The logs are stages, nature's show,
With mushrooms dancing in a row.
History's tangled in the leaves,
Even the breeze plays tricks and weaves.

So sit with me, and let's partake,
Of woodland tales that make you shake.
For in this space, the past is bright,
And laughter echoes through the night.

Sprouts of Recollection

Oh, little sprouts in a line,
You wobble, twist, and try to shine.
Dandelions chuckle from the ground,
While carrots giggle, round and proud.

The sun brings jokes, it's a sunny roast,
As beetle bands give nature a boast.
The daisies sway to the cheerful tunes,
While worms slide in their funny costumes.

Frogs leap, croaking their silly rhymes,
Counting bugs, they lose track of times.
While daisies form a curious crew,
Debating the hues of the morning dew.

All gather 'round this festival of green,
Sharing secrets that have ever been.
In the chaos of roots and weeds,
Life's humor lays in simple deeds.

The Hidden Life of Gnarled Branches

Gnarled branches twist, a wily crew,
Whispering stories only they knew.
With leafy ears, they overhear,
Tree frogs gossip, oh so near.

Rain makes them dance, a wet ballet,
While woodpeckers drum, come out and play!
Rusty old knots hold secrets tight,
As beetles wear jackets, what a sight!

Mice giggle in the tangled wood,
Plotting mischief, as all mice should.
They race and dart, a thrill in the air,
While shadows tease without a care.

So listen close to their nightly chuckles,
In every creak, hear the playful huddles.
Gnarled branches bear witness to the jest,
In nature's arms, we're all a guest.

Journal of the Sylvan Whisperers

In the journal of leaves, stories unfold,
Of cheeky critters, both brave and bold.
With every rustle, a tale is spun,
As rabbits hop, just having fun.

The sunlight scribbles notes on the air,
While chipmunks compete, and they quite dare.
Squirrels plot heists for berries so sweet,
Their antics echo, a comical feat.

Beneath the boughs, friendships bloom,
As fairies sneak past with a gleeful zoom.
Pine cones giggle, rolling down,
As clumsy deer trip through the town.

So join the dance in this woodland cheer,
Every nook and cranny, laughter's near.
In this journal, nature tells her joke,
A family of misfits, in silence, spoke.

Nature's Timekeeper

The trees wear watches, it's true,
With leaves that tick and tock too.
Squirrels debate what hour it is,
While raccoons blame it on the fizz.

Birds sing loudly, their clocks are clear,
Saying, 'Wake up, it's breakfast, dear!'
Time seems slower when you're a snail,
Planning a race - you'll sure fail!

Mushrooms pop like party hats,
Swaying gently with chubby chats.
The sun rolls in, it's half-past fun,
Nature's clockwork has just begun!

So join the dance, let's lose the hour,
With puppets of grass, we'll stomp and tower.
Nature's time is a playful thing,
Full of surprises with every spring!

Stories from the Forest Floor

Under the leaves, secrets are found,
Whispers of critters, all around.
An ant tells tales of yesterday's crumbs,
While mice share dreams of future sums.

A toad croaks stories both big and small,
Of moonlit frogs that dance at the ball.
He says, 'If you hop, you must do it right,
Or risk the chance of a comical fright!'

Fungi argue about who's the coolest,
While elves play tunes, aren't they the fullest?
Old trees gossip about passing deer,
And giggle at each creeping fear.

So grab a seat on the forest floor,
For tales and laughter forevermore.
In the heart of nature, joy's indoors,
With stories aplenty and endless roars!

The Silent Growth

In the hush of night, the plants have talks,
Planting their dreams in their garden socks.
Each shoot a secret, each leaf a laugh,
Plotting their rise on a leafy path.

The flowers giggle when sunlight shows,
Saying, 'Look at me, in my fancy clothes!'
Roots laugh underground, plotting their dance,
With wiggles and jiggles, they take a chance!

The growth is silent, but oh so grand,
With beetles holding a post-it brand.
'Growth spurt today!' says a spry little bud,
Wiggling in soil, creating a flood.

So here's to the fun beneath our feet,
Where everything grows with a rhythm and beat.
Shh now, listen, the garden's delight,
In the silent growth, there's plenty of light!

A Tapestry of Seasons

Spring skips in like it owns the place,
With a daffodil smile and a sunbeam face.
Birds in bow ties, singing so bright,
While blossoms fashion a colorful sight.

Summer rolls in on a beach ball ride,
With sunscreen slathered, it takes a stride.
Picnics and laughter fill up the days,
As nature plays in a sunlit haze.

Autumn wears sweaters and juggles leaves,
Crafting potions from acorns, oh please!
Pumpkins grin wide as harvests align,
While cider is bubbling, a fruity wine.

Winter glides in with a snowman's grin,
Flakes fall like confetti, where to begin?
Hot cocoa and stories by candlelight glow,
Each season's a twist in the nature show.

So here's to the fun, let the seasons play,
Each thread creates joy in its own special way.
A tapestry woven with laughter and cheer,
Nature's grand stage, let's all persevere!

Musings of Maple

In a forest so grand, a maple did think,
About all its friends, with a wink and a blink.
The oaks boast of size, the pines brag of height,
Yet the maple, so modest, just sways in delight.

It chuckles at squirrels, who stash nuts like kings,
And rolls with the laughter of birds and their flings.
Among leaves it finds joy, in colors so bright,
When the autumn breeze dances, oh what a sight!

With a flick of its leaves, the wind starts to play,
As critters come rushing to join in the fray.
A party of nature, no bills to be paid,
Where each critter's welcome, not one will be swayed.

So here's to the tales in the canopy high,
Of funny little moments that flutter on by.
The maple stands proud, a jester on stage,
In a world full of laughter, it turns the next page.

The Light Through the Leaves

Sunshine glimmers, a wink from the sky,
Through leaves that are giggling as breezes float by.
They twinkle in shades, a kaleidoscope show,
Bouncing silly shadows where giggly plants grow.

The rays sneak and peek, play tag with the bark,
Casting silly patterns where creatures embark.
A rabbit once tripped on a patch of bright light,
And fell in a tangle, what a comical sight!

The woodpecker chuckles, a tap-tap of cheer,
While dancing leaf whispers tickle the ear.
A chipmunk joins in, with an acorn parade,
In a groove made of sunshine, they all serenade.

So let's twirl and whirl in this magical glen,
With laughter and light as our favorite pen.
For nature's a showman, a jester quite wise,
In the theater of wonder beneath sunny skies!

A Timeworn Tale

Once a grand tree with reasons to boast,
Sat whispering secrets and popping sweet toast.
It claimed to be ancient, a relic of time,
But lost track of years in its own little rhyme.

An old crow named Clyde would perch on its face,
And tease it with tales of each past, silly race.
"Remember the wind that once whisked you away?"
The tale spun like webs, from night until day!

The tree sighed, then chuckled, recalling that breeze,
Whirling with laughter, it swayed with such ease.
"I shook up my leaves and swayed with great flair,
While squirrels lost acorns without any care!"

As seasons would change, the tree found its throne,
With roots deep in stories and leaves overgrown.
In the tale garden laughing, all ages align,
With the wise, timeworn tree still sipping on wine.

Celebration of Change

In the heart of the woods, we dance with delight,
As leaves turn their jackets from green to bright light.
The crickets are chatting, the fireflies glow,
It's a party in nature, with all in the show.

The birch sheds its skin, while the toad hops with flair,
A tap-dancing turtle brings joy to the air.
With pumpkins all ready for pie-making dreams,
And cider that bubbles, oh how laughter beams!

The winds of October play tricks with our hair,
While nature's confetti rains down everywhere.
With friends by our side, we cherish the scene,
An ode to the whims of the seasonal green!

So raise up your mugs, let's toast to the fun,
To changes and chuckles, our hearts are now one.
For in every season, may laughter arise,
In a festival formed where the earth meets the skies!

Fragments of Flora

In the garden, a plant wears a hat,
The daisies giggle, what's up with that?
A snail in shades slides across the grass,
While punchline petals just shake and laugh.

Bees buzzing jokes with their pollen crew,
A butterfly flutters, says, 'What's the hue?'
The thyme sprigs whisper tales of their past,
As the sun sets down with a wink and a blast.

The flowers throw parties to dance all night,
In bloom's little world, everyone's polite.
But roses play pranks, oh what a tease,
And lilies break out singing with ease.

A potted cactus can't take a joke,
With spikes in the air, it's too hard to poke!
The ivy entwines in a ticklish fight,
As gardening gloves wave, it's pure delight.

Twilight in the Thicket

Amid the twilight, shadows play tricks,
A squirrel debates between two acorns, quick!
One says 'shiny', the other says 'bumpy',
While crickets serenade this night so jumpy.

A raccoon in glasses reads 'How to be Wise'
While a wiseowl rolls its amused eyes.
Fireflies turn on their disco lights,
And ants on a dance floor hold silly fights.

A hedgehog in plaid struts down the lane,
Chasing after dreams like a runaway train.
The trees all giggle, their branches in glee,
As the night sings softly, oh what a spree!

The soundtrack of laughter stretches the dusk,
As frogs leap around, in their green, sassy musk.
A badger wearing boots walks with flair,
While whispering secrets with the cool night air.

Tales of a Timeless Grove

In the grove where giggles happily grow,
A tree with a beard says, 'Hey there, whoa!'
It tells of adventures from times long past,
While the breeze chuckles, so calm, so fast.

The mushrooms hold council with caps in a row,
Debating which fairy has the best glow!
Old roots tell stories all wrinkly and wise,
As the moon peeks through, with her watchful eyes.

A llama in overalls grazes with flair,
Guarding the laughter and fresh woodland air.
The crickets compose symphonies sweet,
While wiggly worms tap dance to the beat.

In this timeless grove where fun never ends,
Trees form a band, tapping branches like friends.
Each leaf is a note, rustling happily clear,
As nature's great choir fills hearts with cheer.

The Journey of the Jumble

In a bag full of goodies, a mix-up in sight,
A pickle meets cookies in a whimsical fight.
The fruits play charades, the veggies just sigh,
While chips tell tall tales of a pie in the sky.

The soda pops fizz, with jokes on a roll,
'Why so fizzy? Just out for a stroll!'
Popcorn's a poet, reciting its rhyme,
As cheese doodles tumble in laughable clime.

A gummy bear rides on a marshmallow horse,
Chasing down laughter with unforeseen force.
The pretzels stand guard, all twisted and proud,
While a chocolate bar's sweetly wrapped in a crowd.

Every snack has a story, a giggle to share,
As they journey together without a care.
In this bag of delights, chaos reigns free,
Feasting on fun, what a sight to see!

www.ingramcontent.com/pod-product-compliance
Lightning Source LLC
Chambersburg PA
CBHW071854160426
43209CB00003B/553